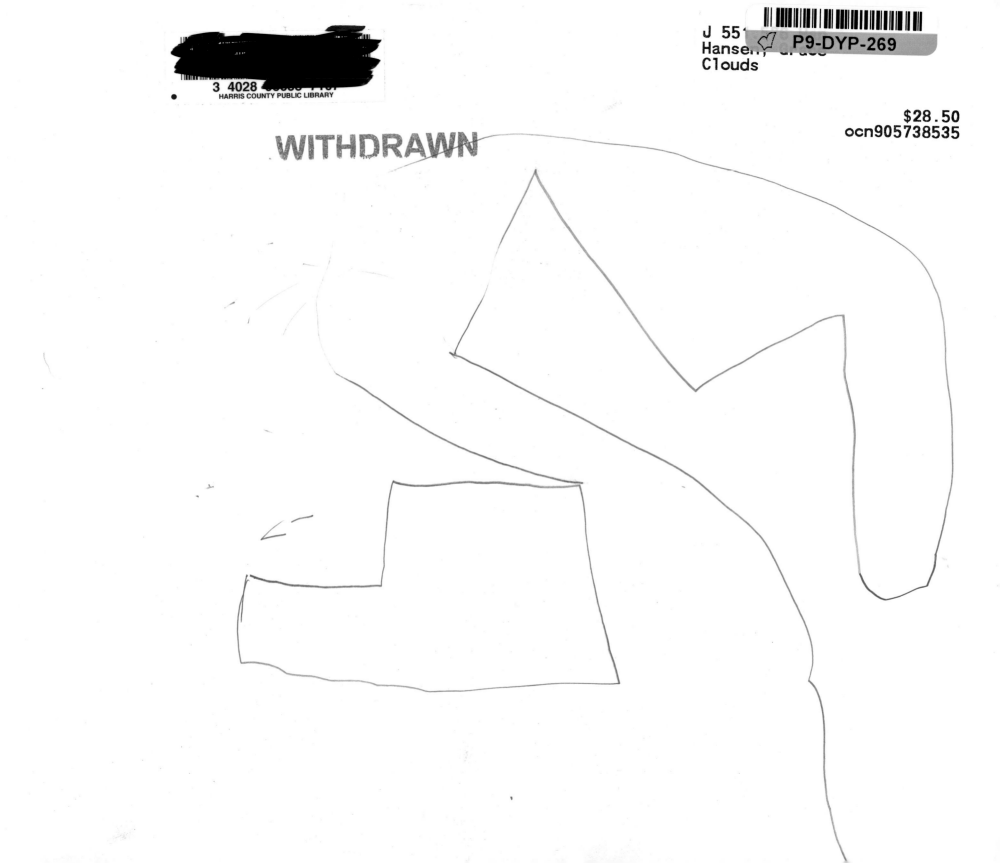

Clouds

by Grace Hansen

Abdo WEATHER Kids

abdopublishing.com

Published by Abdo Kids, a division of ABDO, PO Box 398166, Minneapolis, Minnesota 55439.

Copyright © 2016 by Abdo Consulting Group, Inc. International copyrights reserved in all countries. No part of this book may be reproduced in any form without written permission from the publisher.

Printed in the United States of America, North Mankato, Minnesota.

052015

092015

THIS BOOK CONTAINS RECYCLED MATERIALS

Photo Credits: iStock, Shutterstock

Production Contributors: Teddy Borth, Jennie Forsberg, Grace Hansen

Design Contributors: Laura Rask, Dorothy Toth

Library of Congress Control Number: 2014958416

Cataloging-in-Publication Data

Hansen, Grace.

 Clouds / Grace Hansen.

 p. cm. -- (Weather)

ISBN 978-1-62970-931-4

Includes index.

1. Clouds--Juvenile literature.   I. Title.

551.57'6--dc23

                2014958416

Table of Contents

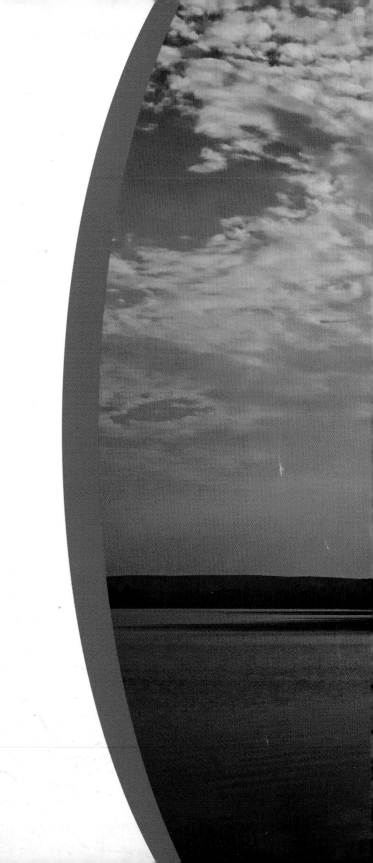

Making Clouds

Clouds are a part of the water cycle. The sun heats water on Earth. Heat makes water **evaporate**.

5

The water goes into the air.

It is now **water vapor**.

Warm air can hold lots of vapor.

Warm air rises. The air cools as it rises. It takes the vapor with it. Cold air cannot hold as much vapor.

The vapor condenses into water droplets. This is called **condensation**.

The vapor must cling to something. Salt, dust, and other things are in the air. These are at the center of each droplet. The many droplets form a cloud.

dust

Different Kinds of Clouds

All clouds form the same way. But they all look different. Fluffy clouds are called cumulus.

14

15

Flat clouds are called stratus. Thin, wispy clouds are called cirrus.

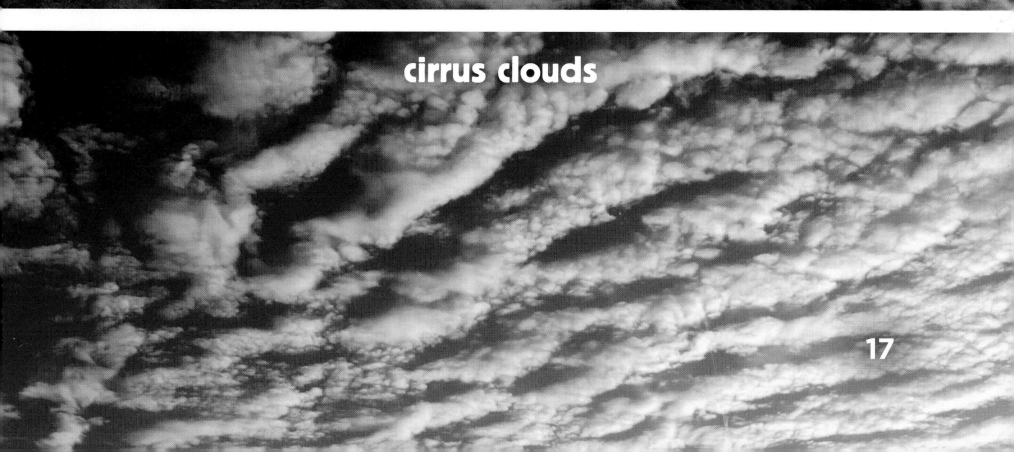

stratus clouds

cirrus clouds

17

Clouds Are Important

Clouds can make rain, snow, and hail. This brings fresh water to Earth.

Clouds **reflect** the sun's light. This helps cool Earth. Clouds also trap the sun's heat. This warms Earth. This **balance** is very important.

How Clouds Form

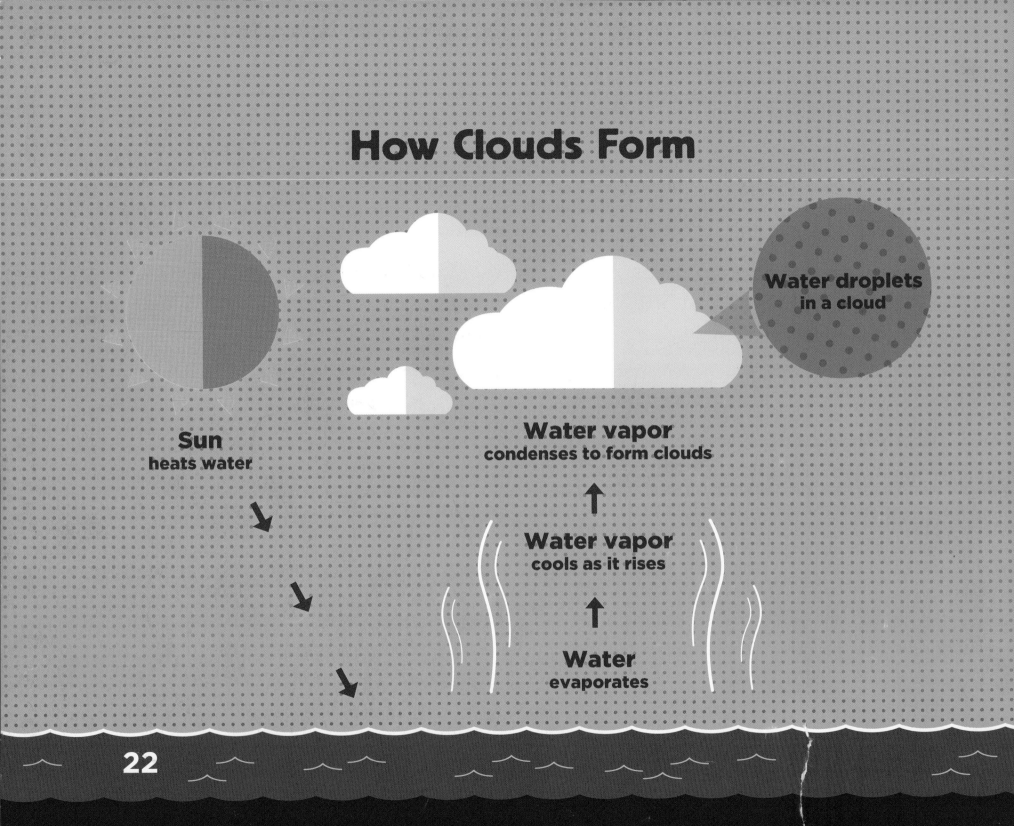

Water droplets
in a cloud

Sun
heats water

Water vapor
condenses to form clouds

Water vapor
cools as it rises

Water
evaporates

Glossary

balance – different and important things that happen in the right amounts.

condensation – the process of condensing. Condensing is to change to a denser form, like from a gas to a solid or a liquid.

evaporation – the process of evaporating. Evaporating is to change from a liquid or solid state into vapor.

reflect – able to shine light back.

water vapor – water in gas form.

Index

abdokids.com

Use this code to log on to abdokids.com and access crafts, games, videos, and more!

Abdo Kids Code:
WCK9314